THE OFFICIAL ICKY POO BOOK

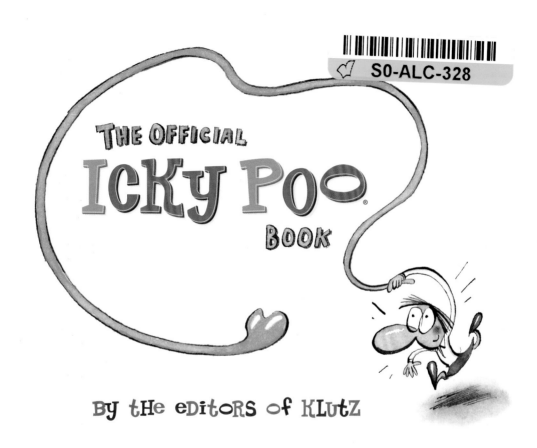

BY THE EDITORS OF KLUTZ

KLUTZ.

THe ICKy Poo StoRy

It all started in John Chen's backyard laboratory.
It was fall, 1976, and Mr. Chen, a research physicist, was noodling around with some odd materials known as "gels." He'd been banished from the kitchen but, with the help of a hotplate and some salvaged equipment, he'd been able to re-establish his research facility in the backyard where, unbeknownst to him or his neighbors, the frontiers of Weird Science were about to be pushed forward in a quantum leap.

Gels are odd mutts in a world of solids, liquids and gases, and they have never attracted enormous research interest — which helps to account for the spartan laboratory conditions Mr. Chen was working with.

As he poked around at his latest effort, **an extremely gooey concoction** that clung devotedly to the bottom of a dish, his first thoughts were those of failure; the stuff looked like it was going to be a mess to clean up. Indeed, it took a half-hour of effort and no less than three rolls of paper towels before Mr. Chen was able to extract the blob and throw it disgustedly in the trash.

It might have been the end. If Icky Poo is ever made into a movie this moment will have to represent its darkest hour.

3

For a full day, the world's one and only sample of Icky Poo rested in Mr. Chen's trash basket, waiting for its short ride into oblivion. But the next day, as Mr. Chen was emptying the trash, he happened to notice something interesting: **The "blob" had taken an imprint of the inside of the dish — right down to the scratches.** This was interesting enough to warrant a little further investigation. The rest of the trash went into the garbage. The blob was saved and taken back inside.

Clearly, the material was "hard set"; i.e., it had memory. Despite yesterday's extraction ordeal, it had managed to remember its shape. That was curious enough, but nothing compared to the next discovery, the one upon which **it would one day stake its claim to the title "Most Disgustingly Appealing Substance in the World."**

The blob, it turned out, was true Weirdness itself. It was a "clean glue"; it stuck, but left no residue.

From a materials science point of view, this was academically interesting. But from any more normal point of view, it was incredible.

Mr. Chen cut off a sample and gave it to his nephew, just to see what the effect would be on the adolescent mind. Predictably, there was an instant bond. But to the inquiring mind willing to go a little deeper, **there is a lot more to do with this amazing stuff than just hold it and scream.**

From the moment Mr. Chen walked into our offices and plopped a sample onto our ceiling fan, we knew what we had to do: Go where no other had gone before. With the sometimes barely controllable help of our local grammar school, we re-named the material "Icky Poo" and then devised 36 activities, each of which relies on the unique properties of John Chen's "elastomeric gelatinous compound."

Care and feeding of Icky Poo

Icky Poo is a mature substance that asks very little of its owner. It needs no batteries, it requires no special handling, there are no moving parts, it's almost completely carefree.

Notice we said "almost."

WHERE CAN I STICK IT?

Icky Poo does have a weakness, a "problem area," almost an obsession — latex paint.

When the rubber molecules in Icky Poo come into contact with the rubber molecules in latex paint — of which there are many — there is **an instant, deep, chemical bond,** most clearly evidenced by a parentally disapproved faint gray "wet" mark left on any latex-painted wall that has been used for target practice.

You can test this unfortunate habit by locating a piece of latex-painted wall that no one will ever see or care about. Then whap your Icky Poo onto it. The attraction is immediate. **Even if your Icky Poo is brand-new clean, there will be a telltale ring-around-the-collar mark on the wall when you pull it off.** Clear evidence of rubber-to-rubber affection.

This wouldn't be a problem except for the fact that latex paint is **the basic wall paint, used almost everywhere on interior walls.** As a result, there is the potential for domestic problems.

Where does all this leave you and your insatiable need to stick our Icky Poo onto things? It just means you have to be a little careful in your choice of stickable surfaces. **The primary rule: Stay away from painted walls.**

Instead, stick with the world of non-latex painted surfaces: furniture, floors, appliances, windows, metal, tile, wood, plastic… etc. Paper (i.e., wallpaper) can also be a problem area, acting like a blotter and pulling out the oil in Icky Poo. But if you move quickly, and don't let your Icky Poo stay on the paper for any length of time, you should be OK.

CAN I TEAR IT?

In a word, yes. If you pull hard enough, Icky Poo will stretch to about 12 times its length… and then, in a heartbreaking moment, it will break. Also, if you ignore these warnings and persist in pulling it out to its maximum stretch, it will begin to show cracks and little tears (Icky Poo age wrinkles). The lesson is: **Be kind to your Icky Poo, never stretch it to its limit,** and it will last a lot longer.

One other prime rule: As we say around here, **dirty Icky Poo is bad Icky Poo.** It won't stick and it leaves dirt wherever it goes. As soon as yours starts to pick up a lot of dirt, lint, etc., take it in for a good washing with soap and water. Once it dries, it'll soon get back to its sticky self.

MISCELLANEOUS CONCERNS

Icky Poo is not for eating or cooking. It is a non-toxic substance but, still, don't make a sandwich out of it. In the same cautionary vein, don't use it to sling heavy or pointed objects around.

GLOSSARY

There are a few activities that are unique to Icky Poo and, as such, they have their own vocabulary. Here they are, along with some instructive illustrations.

ZAPPING

ZAPPING

A natural Icky Poo activity, almost irresistible. **One hand hangs on while the other pulls back and releases.** Most people are reminded of a parallel activity, namely, zapping things with rubber bands (an activity now known as "mini-zapping"). Incidentally, we often double up the paddle rope before we zap anything.

ZINGING

ZINGING

This might be unique to Icky Poo. It's a means of **extending Icky Poo to its full length by just whipping it back and forth.** It works because of its incredible elasticity. Try it. It's much easier done than said.

NEVER zap or zing near someone's face. Icky Poo likes to collect dirt, which is not good for your eyes.

11

Frog Tongue Darts

If you were a frog, this is the way you'd play darts.

1. **Set up your dartboard** on a safe surface like a window or refrigerator door. Put nine of those little sticky squares of paper (Post-it® Notes) in a space about the size of a dartboard. You can also use scraps of paper and tape.

2. About 5 feet (2 meters) in front of the board, install an imaginary "base line" beyond which you can't step. Flip a coin to see who goes first.

3. The object is to **clean the sticky squares off the surface by zapping them** with your paddle rope.

4. Take turns zapping off the sticky squares. If you miss, you lose your turn. If you score, you keep it. Whoever has the most notes when the last one is zapped is the winner.

oscillation Jump rope

This is a three-person game. one to run, two to oscillate.

1. Locate your rope oscillators about 4 or 5 feet (1.5 meters) apart, each holding one end of the rope. (Rope oscillators are people who hold one end of the rope and wave it up and down. Simple job, fancy title.)

2. It's your oscillators' job to **set up a "standing wave" in the rope that's big enough for someone to run through.** To do that, they have to get organized and wave their ends up and down together, in synch. Note that this is different from swinging a jump rope because the motion depends on the elasticity of the Icky Poo.

3. When the rope is going up and down high enough for someone to fit through, **the runner has to make a dash for it.** If she makes it through, she keeps her spot. If she gets nailed by the rope, she trades places with one of the oscillators.

Basic Brown Bag Icky

Two or more can play this game. For every player, get a big brown grocery bag. Everyone puts identical objects into their bag. The best objects are lightweight and big enough to retrieve easily, like small stuffed animals, crumpled-up newspaper balls, sponges or socks.

1. Give yourselves plenty of room. Stand at least 3 feet (1 meter) apart and put your bags in front of you, at least 5 feet (2 meters) away.

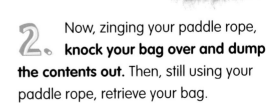

2. Now, zinging your paddle rope, **knock your bag over and dump the contents out.** Then, still using your paddle rope, retrieve your bag.

ALL-YOU-CAN-EAT BROWN BAG ICKY

A variation: Put the bags in the center of a circle. Stand far enough away from them that you won't zing each other when you try to retrieve the bags. Using paddle ropes, everybody dumps out a bag and brings it back near their feet. Now it's a zinging free-for-all. Everybody retrieves stuff until it's all gone. The one with most stuff is the winner.

3. Once you get the bag next to you, **use your paddle rope to go after the contents, piece by piece.** It's OK to use your hands when you get stuff next to your feet. First one to re-fill their bag wins.

POTLUCK BROWN BAG ICKY

A spiced-up variation: Write notes, such as **Give up three of your items** or **Take two items each from the other players,** and put the notes randomly in the bags before starting.

LIZaRD FETCH

If you've ever seen one of those wonders-of-nature movies with lizards that catch flies on their tongues, you'll pick up this game much more quickly.

1. Lay five or six pieces of paper on the floor in a circle with a diameter of, say, 6 or 7 feet (2 meters). **(The bigger the circle, the harder the game.)** Get a partner with a similar fascination with lizards.

2. Stand in the middle of your circle with your paddle rope at the ready.

3. The object of the game is to collect all the sheets off the ground by snagging them with the rope. Note that **you have to sling your rope.** If you can dangle your rope over the paper and "fish" with it, you're too close. Back off. No fair turning around, moving or bending over (this makes the papers behind you pretty difficult to grab).

4. If you miss, you switch with your partner. If you get a paper, you keep your turn. When the last sheet goes, **whoever has the most wins.**

Dragon Fetch

This is competitive Lizard fetch with no holds barred, played for blood. It's not for the faint of heart. You'll need two players, each of whom should be armed with a paddle rope.

1. Players have to separate themselves by 12 to 15 feet (4 to 5 meters). Then, they each set four or five sheets of paper directly in front of them in a small semi-circle, right at their feet.

2. At the starting gun, both players begin **zapping their paddle ropes and snagging the other player's sheets.** (To zap a paddle rope, all you do is hang on to one end and sling the other end out.) You can't move your feet, but when you do snag a sheet, you have to put it down in front of you where it can potentially be grabbed back by the enemy.

3. If the ropes become hopelessly tangled, call an equipment time-out to separate them.

4. If your opponent snags one of your papers, and **if you're quick enough, you can snag it back** before he or she even gets it off the rope.

5. You can declare a winner either of two ways. By playing against the clock, you can stop after 60 seconds to see who has the most sheets, or you can simply play until someone gets all the papers in front of her (not easy).

21

HOLD IT & SCREAM

This is probably the most basic Icky Poo game, and the one that takes the least practice. **All you need to do is open the package to get the idea.** Afterward, there are a couple of subtle variations to it that are definitely worth trying.

THE DISGUSTING HANDSHAKE

A classic game with simple rules. Discreetly **stick the Icky Poo to the palm of your hand and then work the crowd,** pumping flesh. It's like shaking hands with a banana slug. Unforgettable.

THE SHOE THRILL

The same general idea as The Disgusting Handshake; just **insert the Icky Poo into the toe of a shoe** belonging to someone appropriate, and then observe from a safe distance.

"EEEEEEEEEEEEEEEK"

"Close your eyes, open your hand.
Here's a chicken kidney I found."

ICky concentration

A variation on the classic card game of Concentration. You'll need a deck of cards, a steel-trap memory and Robin Hood's deadly eye.

1. Take the deck of cards and arrange them face down on the floor in a circle about the width of your armspan. Locate yourself in the middle and arm yourself with a paddle rope. Your opponent should do the same.

2. Somebody starts. Let's make it you. Zap any card you like. Pull it up, turn it over so that both of you can see it, then return it (by hand) to its place in the circle, face down. **Burn its location and identity into your memory banks.**

3. Your opponent is next. He or she should do the same. At some point, one of you will turn over a card that matches a card that's already been turned over (same number, same color, different suit). When that happens, **yell the following word: "HEY!" If you yell first, you get to try to make the match** by picking up the card's mate. (This pickup can be done by hand, or by Icky Poo zap. Local rules vary.) If your opponent yells first, he or she gets to try.

4. If somebody yells, but then can't find the mate (one chance only), then the turn passes and the other player gets a single chance. If both fail, then the card goes back to its place and you start over.

5. Cards that are successfully matched are put into the matcher's pile. When all the cards are claimed, the winner (naturally) has the larger pile.

Barn Door

This is not really a game so much as an exercise in hysterics. The rules are simple.

1. **Locate a wall that you can safely pelt with Icky Poo.** We have a masonry wall here that is painted with glossy paint. You might have a tile kitchen wall or an outdoor fence or the side of your house… just avoid painted walls and wallpaper.

2. Draw an imaginary line about 10 feet (3 meters) back and line up behind it. Put the (clean) paddle rope in your hand and squeeze it hard. (This is important.)

3. Now relax your hand, **haul back and throw, trying to hit the wall. You'll have to throw pretty hard.**

If it leaves your hand, score **5** points.

If it does not hit you in the foot, score another **5** points.

If it hits the ground, score **10** points.

If it hits the wall at all, score **15** points.

If it hits the wall between eye-height and the top of the wall, **20** extra points.

SCORING EXAMPLES

You throw, it hits the ceiling or flies over the wall. You get 5 points for getting it out of your hand and 5 points for missing your foot.

Total: 10 points.

You throw, it hits the ground. Again, a total of 10 points for getting it out of your hand and missing your foot — plus a bonus of 10 points for hitting the ground.

Total: 20 points.

You throw, it hits your foot. Five points for getting it out of your hand but, since you managed to miss both the ground and the wall, **sorry, no more points.**

ICKY Alien Attack

Pretend you are a Peaceful Planet living under the constant threat of alien invasion. Your only defense is your Icky Poo anti-spaceship emplacement. This is your desperate situation. Here are the rules.

1. Locate yourself in front of a non-painted wall. **This wall is your home planet, which you are attempting to defend.** Opposing you, and standing at a distance of about 15 feet (5 meters), is the alien fleet, consisting of your partner who is holding a well-made paper airplane(s).

2. At a signal, your partner launches his spaceship (paper airplane) toward your home planet (wall). **Your task is to shoot it down by means of a well-aimed Icky Poo zap shot.** If you succeed, you switch places. Points are scored by hits. First to 345,198 is the winner.

Icky poo space wars

This is Icky Alien Attack for two teams. You need at least four people, and more make it better. The object is to keep your opponents' spaceships from landing on your team's planet.

Each side makes paper airplanes out of a different color. (The number of planes you make determines how long the game lasts.) The planes need to be sturdy enough to fly at least 6 feet (2 meters). This game can be played indoors or outdoors, if it's not a windy day.

1. Choose sides. You need at least two people on a side — **one to fly the spaceships and one to defend.** Defenders shoot down opponents' spaceships by zapping them with Icky Poo.

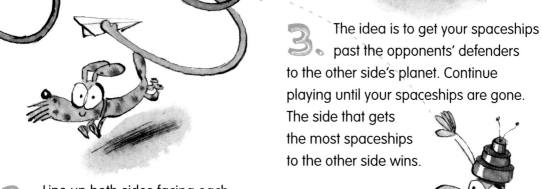

3. The idea is to get your spaceships past the opponents' defenders to the other side's planet. Continue playing until your spaceships are gone. The side that gets the most spaceships to the other side wins.

2. Line up both sides facing each other about 4 feet (1.5 meters) apart. Flyers stand behind defenders. (Defenders, remember, **no zapping until spaceships are in the air.**)

ICKY PARTY GAMES

It has been our experience that one or two paddle ropes of Icky Poo can dominate a birthday party, regardless of how many other presents are available. As a result, we offer the following group games, designed to take advantage of Icky Poo's unique qualities.

Balloon Roundup

A great birthday party game that requires at least two paddle ropes and a collection of birthday party balloons.

1. Put a bunch of balloons in the middle of the floor.

2. Every contestant must equip themselves with a paddle rope. The idea is to **de-populate the floor by zapping the balloons with Icky Poo.** The game begins at a signal and the winner (of course) collects the most balloons. If you have more players than paddle ropes, you might set up a single elimination tournament, and pass around the ropes as need be.

ELECTRIC ICKY

Whereas many of the games in this book rely on the paddle rope's phenomenal elasticity, this one depends on its disgustingness, which is why it's one of the most guaranteed winners here.

1. You'll need a group of at least ten. Your average birthday party should do fine.

2. Everybody sits down cross-legged in two lines, facing each other, an arm's reach apart. **Eyes should be closed. Minds blank.**

3. At the head of the lines sits a referee. He or she should be holding two paddle ropes **all wadded up into two disgusting balls.** Make sure the Icky Poo is clean so it sticks at maximum intensity.

4. All of the players should sit with their hands down on the ground at their sides, palms up. At some unannounced point, the referee will simultaneously place two balls of Icky Poo into the open palms of the players sitting directly next to him. They should be the first players in their respective lines.

5. As soon as he does that, the race is on. The object is to **pass the Icky Poo down the line, hand-to-hand-to-hand.** Eyes must stay closed, and the Icky Poo must touch every hand as it goes down the line. When a player receives the Icky Poo in his open palm (no moving of the hand until the Icky Poo is in it), he then passes it to his other hand and on to the next player.

6. When the last person in a line receives the Icky Poo, that line is finished. But before victory can be claimed, the last person must open her eyes and toss the Icky Poo across the way where it must stick to the chest of the player opposite her.

ICKY picky POO

This is a land-bound version of that esteemed swimming pool game, Marco Polo. It's another great way for a group to play with a single paddle rope. You'll need at least six players and a wide open field with agreed-upon boundaries. How big a field depends on how many players.

1. Someone has to be "it." Once you've settled the occasionally tricky issue of who that's going to be, hand him a paddle rope and blindfold him with a bandana.

2. This game does not permit running, only fast walking. All the other players scatter about. **Whoever's "it" now hollers "icky picky" and everyone else has to holler back "POO."** Based on these sound clues, the "it" player gives chase to the other players (only walking, don't forget).

3. As he's giving chase, he can **swing his paddle rope around in an effort to snag someone.** For safety's sake, all swinging should be below waist level. Other players can dodge or jump as much as they like. But if they get snagged, they have to join the "it" player by putting their hands on his hips, conga line-style.

4. Now another round starts. The only difference is that the person second in line does not have to close her eyes and can holler directions to the paddle rope swinger.

5. As each player is snagged, they **have to join the conga line** until finally, only one person is left. When she is finally snagged, it's time for a new "it" person.

Boa Constrictor Races

This is a variation on an old classic, burlap sack racing. The two main differences: You'll need three people per team and you can skip the burlap sacks.

Position your racers back-to-back-to-back. **Absolutely no talking or laughing allowed.** Wrap them up with your paddle rope. Keep the wraps between shoulders and knees and don't bother with any knots (have racers hold the ends of the rope). At a signal, start your groups off. Keep extending the course as they go along. It's more fun that way.

ICky Limbo

This was inspired by many unsuccessful barbed wire fence crossings. Stretch a paddle rope about 6 inches (15cm) off the ground and attach the ends to something that won't move. (Or you can assign the job to a couple of idle bystanders who need something to do.) Stretch the second paddle rope above it — at about knee level. At a signal, **racers have to run up to this sticky fence and squeeze between the two paddle ropes, cleanly, without touching.** Any touching, and the "stickee" has to start over.

ICKY POO PLOP

This is a cross between musical chairs and the myth of the Sword of Damocles (in which an inhospitable Greek king hung a sword by a thread over a chair at one of his banquets). Our version is a bit more benign and makes an excellent party game.

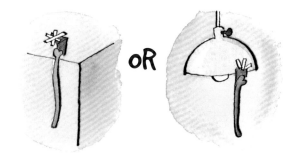

1. You'll need a chair, a paddle rope, a 3x5 card and some tape. Ideally, you'll have a light fixture that you can tape the card to (we did). Otherwise, fold the card in the middle, make an "L" of it, and tape it firmly to the ceiling. (Don't stand on the chair. Ask a grown-up for help if you need it.)

2. Stick your paddle rope to the card as shown. **It should dangle down menacingly.** See how long it takes to fall. If your Icky Poo is clean (and thus sticky) it will take anywhere from 10 to 60 seconds. 5 seconds or less means you need to wash your Icky Poo. Once you've established that your paddle rope falls in a random, but reasonable, period of time, you're ready.

3. The game is simple: **Everybody has to take their chances on being in the chair when the Icky Poo finally plops.** Pick a song that everybody knows, then pick a "volunteer" to start. He has to sit down, sing or recite the first line of the song, and jump up to make room for the next player. (Set an order of players before you start.) The next player sings the next line, jumps up for the next player…

4. Sitters are not allowed to look up, of course, and when someone becomes a "ploppee," they are allowed to re-stick the paddle rope for the next go-round and then get back in line.

♪♫ ON TOP OF SPAGHETTI ♪♫

ICKY POO TAG

This is a sticky variation on the classic game of tag. You'll need to play it outdoors where you've got some running room.

Somebody has to be "it." Let's say that's you. Someone hands you the Icky Poo and then takes off. **Your job is to stick it back on her — or anyone else who's playing.** Any means are fair — you can throw, lash, zap, sling it, anything that works — but you've got to make it stick. Just bouncing it off your victim doesn't count. (Remember, the cleaner the Icky Poo, the stickier it is. If it gets too dirty, you'll have to call an equipment time-out and head for the sink.)

NO HANDS ICKY PASS

A giggles-guaranteed group game. Get several friends to stand in a line or a circle. Then, **without using your hands, pass the poo along to the person next to you,** who will try to get it from you without using his hands, and so on and so on and so on.

The No Game

This is a unique party game that relies on Icky Poo's extraordinary effect on people who are in close physical contact with it. Some people are very anxious to win The No Game, and others, just as anxious to lose it.

And then, of course, there are a few who go back and forth. As you'll soon see, this is probably the best grown-up game in the book.

1. You'll need a group of people together… a classroom of kids, a dinner party of grown-ups, or almost anything in between.

2. The rules are very simple. Someone is selected to start. The Icky Poo is ceremoniously wrapped around her right hand (if she's right-handed; left, if she's left-handed). **Make sure the Icky Poo is at maximum Icky Poo–ness.**

3. The only way the Icky Poo holder can get rid of her Icky Poo is to get someone else to say the word "no" in conversation. Plus, all conversations must begin with a handshaking. **Note that it has to be the word "no."** Synonyms, like "forget it," "you're out of your mind," "negative," etc., don't count.

DOUBLE NEGATIVE VARIATION

At some gatherings, both young and old, you will find those in attendance will love to have the Icky Poo clinging slimily to their hand. If you have one of those groups, and they are just about as common as their opposites, simply make one change in the rules: In order to **take** the Icky Poo from someone, you have to get him to say the word "no" in conversation.

Goalie Icky

A great, perhaps even the greatest, group game with Icky Poo. Works best with groups of about 8 to 14. You'll probably need a small outdoor area, or a play room that has been cleared of breakables and thoroughly approved for high-energy games. The only extra equipment you'll need is a balloon.

1. Break your group up into two teams. Each team has to appoint someone as a goalie. The goalies have to arm themselves with a paddle rope and then plant themselves in the respective back corners of the playing area.

2. Once they've located themselves in their spots, the goalies should draw an imaginary "X" on the ground and cover it with a foot. Henceforward, that foot cannot move.

3. Everyone else gathers in the middle of the room and, at a signal, tosses the balloon up. The object now is simple: **Bat the balloon across the playing area to your goalie who has to zap it** with his Icky Poo, scoring a point. The key rule is no grabbing of the balloon, only batting.

4. That's it. **The rest is a free-for-all. Short of outright mayhem, everything else goes.** You can interfere, hold opponents, whatever works.

Icky Wrap

This is a game for two or more players. Stand 6 feet (2 meters) away from a stop sign or a street sign and, in one swing, **see how many times you can get your Icky Poo paddle rope to wrap around the pole.**

You get 1 point for each revolution. The first one to get 21 points wins.

Important Note: Your Icky Poo has to be clean. If it's not, it won't stick to the pole.

Icky upstairs

Two, or maybe three, people compete in this game, depending on how wide your staircase is. Everybody lines up at the bottom of the stairs. Taking turns, they **zing their Icky Poo paddle ropes up the stairs as high as they will go.** Then players go up the steps to where their Icky Poo landed. The lowest person starts the next round of zinging, and so it goes until the first one gets to the top of the stairs.

Lunch Table Poo

A two-player game designed for lunch tables and that period of time after the trays have been cleared but before the bell rings.

1. You can play with one or two paddle ropes. You'll also need some scraps of paper and a roll of tape or, even better, a pad of Post-it® Notes.

2. Two players sit facing a lunch table. Clear off any debris. Both of you **stick your paper targets on the opposite edge of the lunch table** (the edge neither of you can see — not on the top, not on the bottom, but on the edge). Put ten or so targets in place, scattered along the edge.

3. Both of you go and sit down at the other edge of the table, so neither of you can see the paper targets. Now you're ready.

4. The object of the game is to snag as many targets as possible. **You'll be shooting blind, since you won't be able to see them.** Take turns shooting, five zaps per turn.

5. The best way to snag is to zap your paddle rope, aiming a little over the edge. Do it right and it will wrap around the edge of the table and, if a target is there, snag it and bring it back.

6. Winner, of course, is the one who snags the most targets.

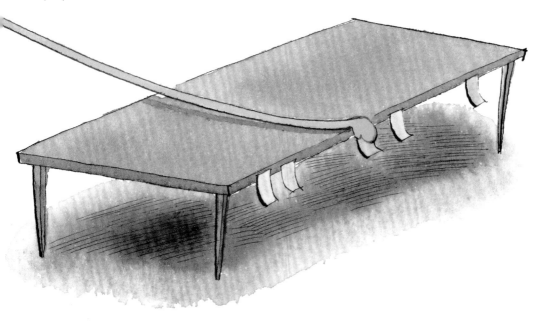

Flypaper trashball

As you've undoubtedly long since discovered, Icky Poo is one of Nature's most misguided missiles. People have been known to stand in front of a large target pinned to a wall, and from arm's length, rear back, let fly, and miss entirely. The wall.

This game circumvents this potential embarrassment by turning the paddle rope into the target, not the missile.

1. Find a place to hang two paddle ropes down to about eye height. Keep them fairly close together. Here in our Icky Poo research facility, we have used a ceiling fan and a light fixture. **Don't stick it straight to the ceiling.** It'll probably leave a mark, and won't stay long enough anyway.

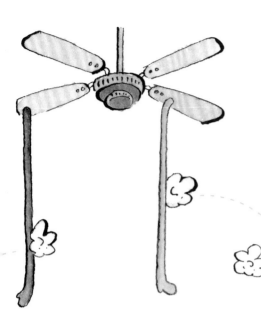

2. Once the two paddle ropes are in place, you've got your target. Now the object is to **just ball up some newspaper (or something similar) and let fly.** Baskets are scored when the paper sticks.

3. You can form teams or not. Set rules about how far back you have to be… etc. Let your imagination fly.

ICKY RETRIEVE

Light-to-Heavy Retrieve

Make sure your Icky is very clean and very sticky for this one. Two people compete in this game. Each of you sets out a course of objects in a line in front of you. The challenge is that the objects get increasingly heavy as you go. You could start with a dollar bill or a feather, then a sock or bandana, then maybe a comic book or a magazine, and finally wind up with something really substantial. Make sure the items in both courses are identical. Zing your Icky Poo to retrieve the objects in order, lightest to heaviest. First to retrieve the heaviest object wins.

Big-to-Small Retrieve

Same idea, but the course consists of papers that decrease in size. Closest to you, a big, easy-to-retrieve piece of paper; next, a little smaller piece; next, smaller, until the one farthest away is miniscule and almost impossible to snag. Zing away, retrieving first the big paper, then the next one, until you get the last itty-bitty one. First one to the itty-bitty one wins. But you have to get the papers in order. No fair skipping.

Retrieve-a-Fortune

Write fortunes or dares on pieces of paper and retrieve them with your Icky Poo. Or, better yet, wrap prizes and retrieve them. No competing here, everyone's a winner.

Fridge Races

This is a chance to pit your paddle rope against someone else's in a contest of raw snail-like speed held on the door of your very own refrigerator.

1. You'll need two clean paddle ropes for this, each with an owner, or handler.

2. Both handlers should stand back a few paces from the chosen refrigerator and, **on a signal, heave their paddle ropes onto its door.** Both have to stick to the door at least as high as some agreed-upon mark. (For example, in our kitchen they have to hit at least as high as the scratch by the top hinge.)

3. If one of the paddle ropes doesn't hit high enough, its owner has to retrieve it and try again (giving the other rope a significant head start).

4. The Icky Poo will creep its way down the door. Winner is the first to the floor.

tactile thrills

Roll a paddle rope into a ball and cover it in plastic wrap. The result? Unsticky icky — which sounds like utter foolishness. Icky Poo without the "icky"? The mind recoils in horror. But just try it. You'll be amazed how appealing these resiliently squeezable little bundles can be.

Afterward, the plastic wrap comes off easily, and your Icky Poo is returned to you in all its wonderfully sticky glory.

- Squeeze your covered Icky Poo for a cheap tactile thrill.

- Take off your shoe and step on it for a solo foot rub.

- Toss it around in a game of Blob Ball Catch.

ICkY-ICkY
SCrub-SCrub

The next time you're in the tub, take your Icky Poo with you. Not only will you clean it up by getting it all wet and soapy, but you'll also **discover a whole new dimension of irresistible sliminess.** You'll be disgusted with yourself for loving it.

ICKY POO CREW

Illustrator: **Hal Mayforth**
Designer: **Kayt de Fever**
Art Director: **Jill Turney**
Zapnik: **Karen Phillips**
Zingster: **Paula Hannigan**
Grand Poo Bah: **John Cassidy**

GRATEFUL ACKNOWLEDGMENTS

John Chen
Simon Goldeen
Martin Gutfeldt
Ninji Martin
Kaja Martin
Rossiter Loren Mikel IV
Bill Olson
Michael Sherman
Scott Stillinger